# The Hallow

***Over 80 ghoulish recipes for appetizers, meals,***

**By Susan Evans**

Other popular books by Susan Evans

Vegetarian Slow Cooker Cookbook:
*Over 75 recipes for meals, soups, stews, desserts, and sides*

Quick & Easy Asian Vegetarian Cookbook:
*Over 50 recipes for stir fries, rice, noodles, and appetizers*

Vegetarian Mediterranean Cookbook:
*Over 50 recipes for appetizers, salads, dips, and main dishes*

Quick & Easy Vegan Desserts Cookbook:
*Over 80 delicious recipes for cakes, cupcakes, brownies, cookies, fudge, pies, candy, and so much more!*

Quick & Easy Vegetarian Rice Cooker Meals:
*Over 50 recipes for breakfast, main dishes, and desserts*

Quick & Easy Rice Cooker Meals:
*Over 60 recipes for breakfast, main dishes, soups, and desserts*

Quick & Easy Microwave Meals:
*Over 50 recipes for breakfast, snacks, meals and desserts*

# ***Free Bonus!***

Would you like to receive one of my cookbooks for free? Just leave me on honest review on Amazon and I will send you a digital version of the cookbook of your choice! All you have to do is email me proof of your review and the desired cookbook and format to susan.evans.author@gmail.com. Thank you for your support, and have fun cooking!

# *INTRODUCTION*

Halloween has always been my favorite time of the year. Although traditionally for kids, it has caught up with Thanksgiving and Christmas as one of the most festive and exciting holidays of the year for grown-ups as well. Nowadays, children and adults both look forward to dressing up in costumes, having fun, and consuming a bit more than they should. With another occasion for friends and families to get-together, this offers more opportunities to entertain and cook some deliciously scary meals.

Whether planning a Halloween-themed dinner party, creating a spooky meal for the family, or wanting to impress at the potluck with a frighteningly delicious and mouth-watering dish, choosing a great Halloween recipe can be stressful and difficult at times. But not anymore. These 80 devilishly good recipes are not only fun and easy to make, but will be a sure hit with both kids and adults alike. Let's get out the cauldron and start cooking!

# ***MEASUREMENT CONVERSIONS***

## Liquid/Volume Measurements (approximate)

1 teaspoon = 1/6 fluid ounce (oz.) = 1/3 tablespoon = 5 ml

1 tablespoon = 1/2 fluid ounce (oz.) = 3 teaspoons = 15 ml

1 fluid ounce (oz.) = 2 tablespoons = 1/8 cup = 30 ml

1/4 cup = 2 fluid ounces (oz.) = 4 tablespoons = 60 ml

1/3 cup = 2⅔ fluid ounces (oz.) = 5 ⅓ tablespoons = 80 ml

1/2 cup = 4 fluid ounces (oz.) = 8 tablespoons = 120 ml

2/3 cup = 5⅓ fluid ounces (oz.) = 10⅔ tablespoons = 160 ml

3/4 cup = 6 fluid ounces (oz.) = 12 tablespoons = 180 ml

7/8 cup = 7 fluid ounces (oz.) = 14 tablespoons = 210 ml

1 cup = 8 fluid ounces (oz.) = 1/2 pint = 240 ml

1 pint = 16 fluid ounces (oz.) = 2 cups = 1/2 quart = 475 ml

1 quart = 4 cups = 32 fluid ounces (oz.) = 2 pints = 950 ml

1 liter = 1.055 quarts = 4.22 cups = 2.11 pints = 1000 ml

1 gallon = 4 quarts = 8 pints = 3.8 liters

## Dry/Weight Measurements (approximate)

1 ounce (oz.) = 30 grams (g)

2 ounces (oz.) = 55 grams (g)

3 ounces (oz.) = 85 grams (g)

1/4 pound (lb.) = 4 ounces (oz.) = 125 grams (g)

1/2 pound (lb.) = 8 ounces (oz.) = 240 grams (g)

3/4 pound (lb.) = 12 ounces (oz.) = 375 grams (g)

1 pound (lb.) = 16 ounces (oz.) = 455 grams (g)

2 pounds (lbs.) = 32 ounces (oz.) = 910 grams (g)

1 kilogram (kg) = 2.2 pounds (lbs.) = 1000 gram (g)

# ***APPETIZERS***

# Creepy Eyeballs

**SERVINGS:** 12
**PREP/ TOTAL TIME:** 40 min. + standing

## Ingredients

- 6 eggs
- 3 cups hot water
- 2 tablespoons red food coloring
- 1 tablespoon white vinegar
- 1/3 cup mayonnaise
- 1/4 cup chopped green onions
- 2 tablespoons minced fresh cilantro
- 2 teaspoons Dijon mustard
- 12 sliced ripe olives
- 1 teaspoon ketchup

## Instructions

1. Place eggs in a large saucepan in a single layer, and add enough cold water to cover by 1 inch. Cover and bring to a boil over high heat. Remove from the heat. Cover and let stand for 15 minutes. Place in ice water until completely cooled. Crack eggs gently, without peeling.
2. Combine 3 cups hot water, food coloring and vinegar in a large bowl. Add eggs, and extra hot water if the eggs are not completely covered. Let stand for 30 minutes. Remove eggs with a slotted spoon and peel.
3. Cut eggs in half along its width. Place yolks in a small bowl and set whites aside. Mash yolks with a fork, stirring in the mayonnaise, onions, cilantro and mustard.
4. Cut a small slice from the bottom of each egg white half to level, and place on a serving platter. Pipe or stuff yolk mixture into center of egg whites. Place an olive slice on each, and fill olives with ketchup. Refrigerate until serving.

# Meaty Worms

**SERVINGS:** 10
**PREP/TOTAL TIME:** 25 min.

## Ingredients

- 1 package of bun-length hot dogs
- Mustard
- Ketchup
- Buns (optional)

## Instructions

1. Cut bun-length hot dogs lengthwise into quarters.
2. Place on grill rack crosswise, and grill uncovered until cooked. They will curve and look wormy.
3. Serve with mustard and ketchup, and buns if desired

# Hairy Witch Fingers

**SERVINGS:** 64
**PREP TIME:** 30 min. + rising
**TOTAL TIME:** 40 min.

## Ingredients

- 3 teaspoons baking yeast
- 1/4 cup warm water (110°F to 115°F)
- 1/2 cup warm milk (110°F to 115°F)
- 1 egg
- 1/4 cup grated Parmesan cheese
- 1/4 cup butter, softened
- 1 tablespoon sugar
- 3/4 teaspoon salt
- 3/4 teaspoon Italian seasoning
- 1/4 teaspoon garlic powder
- 1/4 teaspoon green food coloring
- 2 to 2½ cups all-purpose flour
- 1 egg white, lightly beaten
- 1/4 cup shredded Parmesan cheese
- 1/3 cup sliced almonds
- Marinara or spaghetti sauce

## Instructions

1. In a large bowl, dissolve yeast in warm water. Add milk, egg, grated cheese, butter, sugar, salt, Italian seasoning, garlic powder, food coloring and 1 cup of flour. Beat on medium speed for 2 minutes. Stir in extra flour to form a soft dough.
2. Place on a floured surface, kneading until smooth and elastic, around 6-8 minutes. Place in a greased bowl, turning once to grease top. Cover and let rise in a warm place until doubled, around 45 minutes.
3. Punch down dough and let stand for 10 minutes. Place on a lightly floured surface and divide into 16 pieces. Shape each piece into a 10 inch rope and cut in half. Place 2 inches apart on greased baking sheets. Cover and let rise for 30 minutes.

4. Brush egg white over breadsticks and sprinkle with shredded cheese. Place an almond slice at the tip of each for the nail. Bake at 375° for 8-10 minutes or until lightly browned. Serve warm with marinara sauce.

# Breadstick Bones

**SERVINGS:** 12
**PREP/TOTAL TIME:** 30 min.

## Ingredients

- 1 tube (11 ounces) refrigerated breadsticks
- 1 tablespoon butter, melted
- 2 tablespoons grated Parmesan cheese
- 1/4 teaspoon garlic salt
- 1 can (8 oz.) pizza sauce, heated

## Instructions

1. Unroll and separate breadsticks. Carefully stretch the dough and loosely tie a knot at the ends of each breadstick. Place on cooking sheet and brush with butter.
2. Mix Parmesan cheese and garlic salt; sprinkle over dough. Bake at 375°F for 10-12 minutes or until golden brown. Serve warm with warm "bloody" pizza sauce for dipping.

# Stuffed Cockroaches

**SERVINGS:** 10-15
**PREP/TOTAL TIME:** 1 hour

## Ingredients

- 1/3 cup cream cheese, softened
- 1/4 cup finely chopped walnuts
- 20-30 dates, pitted

## Instructions

1. Mix cream cheese and walnuts together in a small bowl.
2. Slice each date on one side lengthwise to create an opening. Gently fill each date with the cheese and walnut mixture.
3. Pinch the dates closed and place them on a serving plate with the cut sides face down.
4. If desired, place some plastic roaches around the serving plate.

# Crispy Snakes Treats

**SERVINGS:** 8
**PREP TIME:** 15 min.
**TOTAL TIME:** 35 min.

## Ingredients

- 1/2 cup smooth peanut butter
- 3 Tbs butter
- 10-oz package of marshmallows
- Green food coloring
- 4 cups crispy rice cereal
- Cooking spray
- Raisins
- Red fruit leather

## Instructions

1. Melt peanut butter, butter and marshmallows in a large saucepan over low heat, stirring until smooth (about 5 minutes).
2. Remove from heat and stir in a few drops food coloring. Add cereal.
3. Coat a 9x9-inch pan with cooking spray, and spread mixture evenly. Let cool for 20 minutes.
4. Invert pan on a cutting board and remove the cooled square. Cut it into 8 long rectangles.
5. Shape each rectangle into the form of a snake and place 2 raisins for eyes and create a pointed tongue from the fruit leather.

# Fried Mozzarella Eyeballs

**SERVINGS:** 10-12
**PREP/TOTAL TIME:** 25 min.

## Ingredients

- 8 ounce package cream cheese, at room temperature
- 1 cup shredded mozzarella cheese
- 3 green onions, whites only minced
- 3-4 tablespoons Hot Sauce
- 10-15 small black olives
- 1/4 teaspoon kosher salt
- 1/2 cup flour
- 2 eggs
- 1 cup panko bread crumbs
- 3 cups canola oil
- Marinara sauce

## Instructions

1. Blend cream cheese, mozzarella cheese and whites of the green onions in a medium bowl. Scoop cheese mixture with an ice cream scoop and level off the top. Place olive in the middle of the cheese with the hole side up. Fill hole with hot sauce then cover with a spoonful of cream cheese mixture. Mold into a ball and sprinkle more hot sauce. Repeat with the rest of the cheese.
2. In a small saucepan or deep fryer, heat oil to 350°F.
3. Gather three shallow bowls and place flour in one bowl, whisk eggs in another bowl and place panko bread crumbs in remaining bowl. Dig up a cream cheese ball first in flour, then egg and then in panko. Repeat flour, egg and panko steps 2 more times. Set aside and repeat with the rest of the cheese balls.
4. Fry cheese balls in batches of three or four at a time for about 2 minutes or until golden brown. Drain on paper towels. Slice in half or serve whole with marinara sauce on the side.

# Bloody Guts Dip

**SERVINGS:** 16
**PREP/ TOTAL TIME:** 15 min.

## Ingredients

- 2 cups chopped fresh or frozen cranberries
- 1 cup packed brown sugar
- 1/2 cup honey
- 1/4 cup water
- 1 cup Dijon mustard

## Instructions

1. In a small saucepan, combine cranberries, brown sugar, honey and water. Bring to a boil. Cook and stir for 5 minutes or until thickened. Remove from the heat and let it slightly cool.
2. Stir in mustard.
3. Refrigerate until serving.

# Bloody Skewered Fingers

**SERVINGS:** 10
**PREP:** 25 min.
**TOTAL TIME:** 45 min.

## Ingredients

- 1 package of mini sausage links
- 1 packet of tortilla bread
- Ketchup

You'll also need:

- 1 package of toothpicks/skewers

## Instructions

1. Preheat the oven to 300°F.
2. With a knife, cut a sliver off one end of each sausage to make it look like the nail of a finger.
3. Cut the tortilla into thin 1/4 inch wide strips.
4. Wrap the bottom of the finger sausages with the tortilla to make it look like bandages.
5. Bake in the oven for 20 minutes at 300°F.
6. Take out the sausages once they are brown and let them cool slightly.
7. With a small spoon, paint each fingernail with ketchup to make it look bloody.
8. Insert toothpicks or skewers into the bandaged end and place on serving dish.
9. Fill a small bowl with ketchup for bloody dip.

# Slices of Bone

**SERVINGS:** 64

**PREP/ TOTAL TIME:** 25 min. + chilling

## Ingredients

- 1/2 cup mayonnaise
- 1 package (3 ounces) cream cheese, softened
- 2 tablespoons each finely chopped celery, green pepper and onion
- 1 tablespoon lemon juice
- 1 teaspoon ground mustard
- 1 teaspoon Worcestershire sauce
- 1/8 teaspoon lemon-pepper seasoning
- 1/8 to 1/4 teaspoon hot pepper sauce
- 1½ cups cooked or canned crabmeat, drained, flaked and cartilage removed
- 4 flour tortillas (10 inches)

## Instructions

1. Beat mayonnaise and cream cheese in a large bowl until smooth. Add celery, green pepper, onion, lemon juice, mustard, Worcestershire sauce, lemon-pepper and hot pepper sauce. Stir in crabmeat.
2. Spread about 1/2 cup filling over each tortilla. Tightly roll and wrap in plastic wrap. Refrigerate for 2 hours or until chilled. Cut into 1/2 inch slices.

# Stuffed Potato Ghosts

**SERVINGS:** 40
**PREP TIME:** 1½ hours
**TOTAL TIME:** 1 hour 40 min.

## Ingredients

- 2 pounds fingerling potatoes
- 1 large baking potato
- 1/3 cup sour cream
- 2 ounces cream cheese, softened
- 1 tablespoon butter
- 1/4 teaspoon salt
- 1/8 teaspoon pepper
- 7 thin slices Monterey Jack cheese
- 1 tablespoon chopped ripe olives
- 2 green onions, thinly sliced

## Instructions

1. Bake potatoes at 350°F for 40-45 minutes or until tender and set aside.
2. Pierce baking potato with a fork a few times. Microwave for 6-7 minutes or until tender. Cut in half, scoop out pulp and discard shell. Place the pulp in a small bowl and mash. Stir in the sour cream, cream cheese, butter, salt and pepper until smooth.
3. Cut each fingerling in half lengthwise. Spoon 1 tablespoon mashed potato mixture over each potato half and place on a foil-lined baking sheet.
4. Cut each cheese slice into six rectangles, and place one on each stuffed potato. Bake at 350°F for 10-11 minutes or until cheese is melted and potatoes are heated through. Place olives and green onions for eyes and mouths.

# Worms and Dirt

**SERVINGS:** 10
**PREP/TOTAL TIME:** 20 min.

## Ingredients

- 8 hot-dogs
- 2 (15-ounce) cans black beans

## Instructions

1. Slice hot-dogs lengthwise into 1/2-inch-thick strips.
2. Drain and chop the black beans.
3. Bring a large pot of water to a boil over high heat. Reduce heat to a simmer. Add hot dogs and simmer until they curl. Drain the water.
4. Place black beans in a serving bowl and top with curled hot dogs. Tuck in the hot dogs to make it appear as worms coming from the dirt
5. Serve immediately.

# Pepper Popper Monster Fingers

**SERVINGS:** 24
**PREP TIME:** 40 min.
**TOTAL TIME:** 1 hour

## Ingredients

- 1 package (8 ounces) cream cheese, softened
- 1 cup (4 ounces) shredded sharp cheddar cheese
- 1 cup (4 ounces) shredded Monterey Jack cheese
- 6 bacon strips, cooked and crumbled
- 1/4 teaspoon garlic powder
- 1/4 teaspoon chili powder
- 12 medium jalapeno peppers, stems removed, halved lengthwise and seeded
- 1/2 cup dry bread crumbs
- 2 tablespoons ketchup
- 1/4 cup sliced almonds

## Instructions

1. In a large mixing bowl, combine the cheeses, bacon and seasonings. Spoon 1 tablespoonful into each pepper half. Press the tops of each stuffed pepper into bread crumbs.
2. Place a dab of ketchup at the end of each pepper popper and add a sliced almond for the fingernail.
3. Place all the fingers on baking sheet lined with aluminium foil. Bake, uncovered, at 325°F for 20-25 minutes or until golden brown.
4. Serve hot.

# Bite-Sized Ghost Pizzas

**SERVINGS:** 30
**PREP/TOTAL TIME:** 25min.

## Ingredients

- 2 tubes (12 ounces each) refrigerated buttermilk biscuits
- 1 can (8 ounces) tomato sauce
- 1½ teaspoons dried minced onion
- 1 teaspoon dried oregano
- 1 teaspoon dried basil
- 1/8 teaspoon garlic powder
- 20 slices Skim Mozzarella Cheese
- Sliced ripe olives

## Instructions

1. Preheat oven to 400°F. Roll biscuits into 2½ inch circles and place on greased baking sheets.
2. Combine tomato sauce, onion, oregano, basil and garlic powder in a small bowl, and spread over biscuits. Bake 8-10 minutes or until edges are lightly browned.
3. With a knife or a small ghost-shaped cookie cutter, cut a ghost out of each cheese slice. Immediately place a ghost over each pizza; adding olives for the eyes.

# Devils on Horseback

**SERVINGS:** 8
**PREP TIME:** 15 min.
**TOTAL TIME:** 30 min.

## Ingredients

- 24 pitted prunes
- 1/3 cup crumbled blue cheese
- 12 strips of bacon, cut in half crosswise
- 24 Toothpicks

## Instructions

1. Preheat broiler to high. Soak 24 toothpicks in a bowl of water for 15 minutes. Spray cooking spray on a large, rimmed baking sheet and place a wire rack on top.
2. Cut prunes in half lengthwise, without cutting all the way through. Place some cheese in center of each prune, where the pit was removed. Wrap each prune with bacon, secured with toothpick.
3. Broil for 10 to 12 minutes and turn halfway through.

# Slithery Snake Sandwich

**SERVINGS:** 16
**PREP TIME:** 30 min.
**TOTAL TIME:** 2 hours

## Ingredients

- Cornmeal for dusting
- 3 (1 lb.) loaves frozen bread dough, thawed
- 2 green, pimento-stuffed olives
- 1/2 cup plus 2 Tbsp. olive oil
- 2 (12 oz.) jars roasted red and yellow peppers, in oil
- 3 large celery ribs, halved lengthwise and thinly sliced crosswise
- 2 cups pitted black and green olives, coarsely chopped
- 1/4 cup capers, coarsely chopped
- 1/2 teaspoon red pepper flakes
- 3 ounces arugula
- 1 pound thinly sliced prosciutto
- 3 pounds fresh mozzarella, sliced
- 1/4 large red pepper

## Instructions

1. Cover large (12x18x2 inch) baking pan with parchment, lightly dusting with cornmeal. On a floured surface, combine dough and form a long, curvy snake shape. Place the snake on pan. Push two olives into head for eyes. Cut V-shaped scales down back. Brush dough with oil. Cover with plastic wrap and let rise until doubled in size, around an hour. Preheat oven to 350°F. Bake until crust is golden, about 30 to 40 minutes. Cool in pan on rack.
2. Remove roasted peppers from jars and set aside. Add olive oil to the oil from peppers to make a cup. Combine oil, celery, olives, capers and red pepper flakes in a small bowl.
3. Slice the loaf horizontally. Place bottom half on tray arranging arugula leaves on it. Layer prosciutto and mozzarella and top with roasted red peppers. Spoon on olive relish and replace top.
4. With a knife, cut a forked tongue shape from red pepper and place at the head of the snake sandwich.

# Spider Bagel Pizzas

**SERVINGS:** 8
**PREP TIME:** 30 min.
**TOTAL TIME:** 1 hour

## Ingredients

- 1 28 oz. can crushed tomatoes
- 2 tablespoons extra-virgin olive oil
- 4 cloves garlic, chopped
- 1 tablespoon chopped fresh oregano or 1 tsp. dried
- Pinch of crushed red pepper
- Salt and pepper
- 8 whole-wheat or regular mini bagels, sliced in half crosswise
- 6 ounces shredded mozzarella
- 8 pitted large black olives
- 8 pitted large green olives

## Instructions

1. Preheat oven to 350°F. Mix tomatoes, oil, garlic, oregano, crushed red pepper, and 1/2 tsp. of salt and pepper in a large pan, Bring to a boil over high heat. Reduce heat to low and simmer, stirring occasionally, until sauce is slightly thick, about 20 minutes.
2. Place bagel halves on a parchment-lined baking sheet. Spread 2 tablespoon of sauce onto each bagel half. Top each with 1 rounded tablespoon shredded cheese.
3. Slice 1 olive in half lengthwise. Place 1 olive half, cut side down, in center of a bagel half for the spider body. Slice remaining olive half into 8 thin crescents to make 8 spider legs. Arrange 4 legs on each side of body to complete spider. Repeat for all bagel pizzas.
4. Bake pizzas until toasted and cheese has melted, around 10 to 12 minutes.
5. Serve hot.

# Scary Brain Shrimp Cocktail

**SERVINGS:** 12
**PREP/TOTAL TIME:** 25 min. + chilling

## Ingredients

- 3 pounds frozen cooked medium shrimp (with tails), thawed and drained well
- 1/4 cup roasted red sweet peppers, cut into 1/4-inch thick strips
- 1 cup chicken broth
- 1 teaspoon unflavored gelatin
- 1½ teaspoons finely shredded lemon peel
- 1/4 cup lemon juice
- 3 tablespoons tomato paste
- 1 tablespoon honey
- 3 cloves garlic, minced
- 1/2 teaspoon salt
- 1/2 teaspoon ground ginger
- 1/4 teaspoon cayenne pepper

## Instructions

1. In a 1½ quart glass bowl, around 3 inches high, arrange shrimps in a circle with the tails toward the center. Make a flat layer in the bottom of the bowl, with only the round backs of the shrimp visible from the outside of the bowl. Repeat shrimp layers until bowl is full, pressing down every few layers. As you fill up the bowl, place roasted red pepper strips between and around shrimp to form the brain blood vessels. Make sure to look through the glass sides to makes sure they are visible. After filling the bowl, press down firmly with a plate that fits in the bowl and set aside.
2. In a small saucepan combine chicken broth and unflavored gelatin and let stand for 5 minutes. Cook and stir over medium heat until gelatin has dissolved. Whisk in lemon peel, lemon juice, tomato paste, honey, garlic, salt, ginger, and cayenne pepper until combined. Pour mixture over shrimp in bowl. Cover and chill at least 5 hours or overnight.
3. To remove from the mold, place bowl in a sink filled with warm water for several seconds. Invert a large plate with sides over bowl. Invert

both the plate and bowl together and remove bowl. Cover and chill until needed.

# Crescent Mummy Dogs

**SERVINGS:** 10
**PREP TIME:** 10 min.
**TOTAL TIME:** 25 min.

## Ingredients

- 1 can (8 oz.) refrigerated crescent dinner rolls, or 1 can (8 oz.) refrigerated Crescent Dough Sheet
- 2½ slices (2.5 oz.) American cheese, quartered
- 10 large hot dogs
- Cooking spray
- Mustard or ketchup

## Instructions

1. If using crescent rolls: Unroll dough; separate at perforations, and create 4 rectangles. Press perforations to seal. If using the dough sheet: Unroll dough and cut into 4 rectangles.
2. With knife cut each rectangle lengthwise into 10 pieces, making a total of 40 pieces of dough. Slice cheese slices into quarters, and cut the 1/2 slice of cheese in in half).
3. Wrap 4 pieces of dough around each hot dog and 1/4 slice of cheese to make it look like bandages, stretching dough slightly covering the hot dog completely. About 1/2 inch from one end of each hot dog, separate the bandages to leave room for a face. On an ungreased large cookie sheet, place cheese side down and spray dough lightly with cooking spray.
4. Bake 13 to 17 minutes or until dough is light golden brown and hot dogs are hot. Draw a face with mustard or ketchup.

# Monster Phlegm

**SERVINGS:** 10
**PREP/TOTAL TIME:** 5 min.

## Ingredients

- 2 dozen oysters, shucked, juices reserved
- Cocktail Sauce

## Instructions

1. Place oysters and their juices in a tall glass.
2. Serve with cocktail sauce.

# Dragon Claws and Blood

**SERVINGS:** 6
**PREP/TOTAL TIME:** 25 min.

## Ingredients

- 10 cups water
- 1 teaspoon salt
- 1 pound uncooked medium shrimp, peeled and deveined
- 1 cup ketchup
- 2 tablespoons lemon juice
- 2 teaspoons grated lemon peel
- 4 teaspoons prepared horseradish
- 1/4 teaspoon Worcestershire sauce
- 1/8 to 1/4 teaspoon hot pepper sauce
- Lemon wedges

## Instructions

1. In a large saucepan, combine water and salt. Bring to a boil. Add shrimp. Reduce heat and simmer uncovered for 2-3 minutes or until shrimp turns pink, stirring occasionally. Drain. Cool in ice water and drain again. Refrigerate until serving.
2. In a small bowl, combine ketchup, lemon juice, peel, horseradish, Worcestershire sauce and pepper sauce. On a serving platter, arrange shrimp in groups of three to look like the claws of a dragon.
3. Serve with sauce and garnish with lemon wedges.

# Spooky Mummy Brie

**SERVINGS:** 10
**PREP/TOTAL TIME:** 30 min.

## Ingredients

- 1 package (17.3 ounces) frozen puff pastry, thawed
- 1/4 cup apricot jam
- 1 round (13.2 ounces) Brie cheese
- 1 large egg
- 1 tablespoon water
- Apple slices
- 2 dried cranberries or raisins

## Instructions

1. Preheat oven to 400°F. Unfold a sheet of puff pastry. Roll pastry into a 14 inch square on a lightly floured surface. Cut off corners and make a circle. Spread jam into a 4½ inch circle in center of pastry. Place Brie on top and fold pastry over cheese and pinch edges to seal. Beat egg and water and brush over pastry.
2. Place on an ungreased baking sheet, seam side down. Roll remaining pastry into a 14-in. square. Cut four 1 inch strips, cutting strips in half crosswise. Layer strips over Brie. Bake 20-25 minutes or until golden brown.
3. Cut two circles from apple slices to resemble eyes and place on top of brie. Top each apple circle with a dried cranberry.
4. Serve warm.

# Frankenstein Guacamole

**SERVINGS:** 8
**PREP/TOTAL TIME:** 15 min.

## Ingredients

- 3 medium ripe avocados, peeled and cubed
- 1/4 cup finely chopped onion
- 1/4 cup minced fresh cilantro
- 2 tablespoons lime juice
- 1/8 teaspoon salt
- Blue tortilla chips
- 2 tablespoons sour cream
- 1/2 cup refried black beans
- 1/4 cup ripe olives, sliced

## Instructions

1. Mash avocado with a fork in a small bowl. Stir in onion, cilantro, lime juice and salt.
2. Spoon guacamole onto a large platter and form into a rectangle.
3. Place chips near the top of Frankenstein's head, with triangles pointing down.
4. Add the two tablespoons of sour cream to represent the white of eyeballs, and place an olive to represent the pupils.
5. Combine the beans and the rest of the olives. Use the mix to shape into a mouth.

# Pretzel Witch Brooms

**SERVINGS:** 2-4
**PREP/TOTAL TIME:** 20 min.

## Ingredients

- 12 Slices of Cheese
- 12 Pretzel sticks
- 12 Fresh Chive

## Instructions

1. Fold each cheese slice and with a pair of scissors, cut the bottom to create fringes of the broom.
2. Roll the slice of cheese around a pretzel stick having the fringes looking down.
3. Knot some chives around the cheese to hold it in place.

# Green Cheese Frankenstein

**SERVINGS:** 12
**PREP/ TOTAL TIME:** 45 min. + chilling

## Ingredients

- 2 packages (8 ounces each) cream cheese, softened
- 1/4 cup mayonnaise
- 1 tablespoon Worcestershire sauce
- 1 teaspoon hot pepper sauce
- 2 cups (8 ounces) shredded cheddar cheese
- 6 bacon strips, cooked and crumbled
- 3 green onions, thinly sliced
- 2 cartons (4 ounces each) whipped cream cheese
- Moss-green paste food coloring
- 1 can (4¼ ounces) chopped ripe olives, drained
- 2 pepperoncini
- 3 colossal ripe olives
- 2 slices peeled parsnip
- Black decorating gel
- 1 pretzel rod
- 1 small cucumber
- Assorted fresh vegetables

## Instructions

1. In a large bowl, beat the cream cheese, mayonnaise, Worcestershire sauce and pepper sauce until smooth. Stir in the cheddar cheese, bacon and onions. Shape into a 5x4x3 inch rectangle and wrap in plastic wrap. Refrigerate until chilled.
2. Unwrap rectangle and place on a serving platter with a 3 inch side on top. Tint whipped cream cheese green and spread over top and sides of rectangle.
3. Add chopped ripe olives for hair on top and pepperoncinis for the ears. Cut one colossal olive in half; add parsnip slices and olive halves for the eyes. With black decorating gel, pipe the eyebrows, mouth, and stitches.

4. Break pretzel rod in half; add a colossal olive to each end. Press into sides of head for bolts. Cut a small piece from end of cucumber for the nose.
5. Serve with vegetables.

# Vampire Lips

**SERVINGS:** 8
**PREP/ TOTAL TIME:** 20 min.

## Ingredients

- 1 medium red apple
- 1 teaspoon lemon juice
- 1/4 cup chunky peanut butter
- 2 tablespoons reduced-fat cream cheese
- 1/8 teaspoon ground cinnamon
- Miniature marshmallows

## Instructions

1. Cut apple into 16 wedges and toss with lemon juice.
2. In a small bowl, mix peanut butter, cream cheese and cinnamon until blended. Spread about 2 teaspoons onto one side of half of the apple slices. Top each with a second slice, pressing together to form lips. Press marshmallows onto peanut butter for vampire teeth. Refrigerate until serving.

# Yummy Finger Sandwiches

**SERVINGS:** 18
**PREP/ TOTAL TIME:** 30 min.

## Ingredients

- 12 ounces cream cheese, softened
- 1/2 cup finely chopped almonds, toasted
- 1/4 cup chopped green onions
- 2 tablespoons minced fresh parsley
- 1 teaspoon lemon juice
- Dash salt and pepper
- 12 thin slices white sandwich bread, crusts removed
- 9 medium carrots, peeled
- Additional cream cheese
- 36 almond slices

## Instructions

1. In a small bowl, beat the cream cheese, chopped almonds, onions, parsley, lemon juice, salt and pepper until blended. Spread over bread slices. Cut each into three 1 inch wide strips.
2. Cut carrots in half width-wise, then cut in half length-wise. Using a vegetable peeler, shape carrot pieces into fingers. Using a small amount of additional cream cheese, attach an almond slice to the tip of each finger for the finger nail. Place a finger on top of each sandwich.

# Spider Slider Burgers

**SERVINGS:** 12
**PREP TIME:** 20 min.
**TOTAL TIME:** 45 min.

## Ingredients

- 2 large sweet potatoes (about 12 ounces each)
- 1/2 teaspoon salt
- 1/4 teaspoon ground cumin
- 1/4 teaspoon dried thyme
- 1/8 teaspoon ground cinnamon
- 1/8 teaspoon pepper
- 1/4 cup canola oil
- 1 pound ground beef
- 1/4 cup dried minced onion
- 1/2 teaspoon seasoned salt
- 6 slices process American cheese
- 12 dinner rolls, split
- 24 pimiento-stuffed olive slices

## Instructions

1. Adjust oven racks to upper-middle and lower-middle position. Preheat oven to 400°F. Peel and cut sweet potatoes into 1/4 inch. Julienne strips. Place in a greased 15x10x1 inch baking pan. Mix salt, cumin, thyme, cinnamon and pepper. Drizzle sweet potatoes with oil and sprinkle with spice mixture. Toss to coat.
2. Bake on bottom oven rack for 25-30 minutes or until golden brown and tender, turning once.
3. In a large bowl, combine beef, onion and seasoned salt, mixing lightly but thoroughly. Press onto bottom of a greased 13x9 inch baking dish. Bake on top oven rack 15-20 minutes or until a thermometer reads 160°F.
4. Drain fat from baking dish and place cheese slices evenly over meat. Bake 2-3 minutes or until cheese is melted. Cut into 12 patties.
5. Place one patty on each roll bottom. Arrange eight fries to form spider legs. Place top of bun. Press two olive slices onto cheese for the eyes.

# Yummy Worm Sandwiches

**SERVINGS:** 6
**PREP/ TOTAL TIME:** 20 min.

## Ingredients

- 1 package (16 ounces) hot dogs
- 1 tablespoon canola oil
- 1/2 cup ketchup
- 1 tablespoon brown sugar
- 2 teaspoons Worcestershire sauce
- 1/2 teaspoon spicy brown mustard
- 6 hamburger buns, split

## Instructions

1. Cut each hot dog into eight strips. In a large skillet, sauté hot dogs in oil until golden brown.
2. Stir in the ketchup, brown sugar, Worcestershire sauce, and mustard. Heat through.
3. Serve on buns.

# Mummy Bread Spinach Dip

**SERVINGS:** 18
**PREP TIME:** 25 min.
**TOTAL TIME:** 2½ hours

## Ingredients

- 1 pkg. (16 oz.) frozen pizza dough, thawed
- 1 egg, beaten
- 2 sticks mozzarella string cheese
- 2 black olive slices
- 1 cup Reduced Fat or Light Sour Cream
- 1/4 cup Lite Ranch Dressing
- 1 pkg. (10 oz.) frozen chopped spinach, thawed, well drained
- 1 green onion, sliced
- 1/2 cup finely chopped red peppers
- 1/4 cup KRAFT Grated Parmesan Cheese
- 1/4 tsp. ground black pepper
- 1 package thin wheat snack crackers

## Instructions

1. Pat dough into 12x6 inch oval on baking sheet sprayed with cooking spray. About 3 inches from one end of oval, indent dough for the head of the mummy. Let rise in warm place 20 minutes or until doubled in volume.
2. Heat oven to 375ºF. Brush dough with egg. Bake 18 to 20 min. or until bread is golden brown and when tapped lightly, sounds hollow. Pull apart string cheese to make about 16 strips and arrange on bread to look like a mummy's wrapping. Bake 1 to 2 minutes or just until cheese is melted. Cool slightly. Press olive slices into bread for the mummy's eyes and cool completely.
3. Mix sour cream and dressing in medium bowl until blended. Stir in the next 5 ingredients. Refrigerate 30 minutes or until ready to serve.
4. Use sharp knife to remove bread from top of mummy's body. Scoop out bread from center and leave a thin shell on bottom and side.

Reserve bread top, and either discard removed bread or reserve for something else. Fill bread with spinach dip just before serving and cover with top of bread. Serve with crackers.

# Jack-O-Lantern Stuffed Peppers

**SERVINGS:** 4-6
**PREP TIME:** 25 min.
**TOTAL TIME:** 1½ hours

## Ingredients

- 6 bell peppers, any color
- 1 pound ground beef
- 1 egg
- 4 slices whole wheat bread, cubed
- 1 small onion, chopped
- 1 small tomato, diced
- 2 cloves garlic, minced
- 1/2 cup chili sauce
- 1/4 cup prepared yellow mustard
- 3 tablespoons Worcestershire sauce
- 1/4 teaspoon salt
- 1/4 teaspoon pepper

## Instructions

1. Preheat oven to 350°F. Grease an 8x8 inch baking dish.
2. Combine the ground beef, egg, bread cubes, onion, tomato, garlic, chili sauce, mustard, Worcestershire sauce, salt, and pepper in a bowl.
3. Wash the peppers, and cut jack-o'-lantern faces into the peppers with a sharp paring knife. Slice off the tops of the peppers, and scoop out the seeds and cores. Stuff the peppers lightly with the beef stuffing. Place them into the prepared baking dish so they lean against each other.
4. Bake in the preheated oven until the peppers are tender and the stuffing is cooked through and juicy, about 1 hour.

# *ENTREES*

# Oozy Eyeballs and Spaghetti

**SERVINGS:** 8
**PREP TIME:** 20 min.
**TOTAL TIME:** 45 min.

## Ingredients

- 2 lb. lean ground beef
- 1 pkg. (6 oz.) Stuffing Mix for Chicken
- 1 cup water
- 2 eggs
- 1 jar (24 oz.) spaghetti sauce, divided
- 4 sticks of Mozzarella string cheese, cut into quarters
- 4 large pitted black olives, cut into 4 slices each
- 1 pkg. (1 lb.) spaghetti, uncooked

## Instructions

1. Heat oven to 375°F.
2. Mix meat, stuffing mix, water, eggs and 1/4 cup spaghetti sauce. Form into 16 (2 inch) meatballs. Insert a cheese piece into top of each meatball, with end of cheese piece just visible at top. Place on baking sheet. Top each with olive slice to make it look like an eyeball.
3. Bake 20 to 25 minutes or until meatballs are done a 160°F. Meanwhile, cook spaghetti as directed on package, without adding salt and heat remaining spaghetti sauce as directed on jar.
4. Drain spaghetti and serve topped with meatballs and sauce.

# Spicy Skeleton Ribs

**SERVINGS:** 28
**PREP TIME:** 25 min.
**TOTAL TIME:** 1 hour 10 min.

## Ingredients

- 4 cups diced cooked chicken breast
- 1¼ cups water
- 1/4 cup tomato paste
- 2 tablespoons paprika
- 2 tablespoons lime juice
- 1½ teaspoons onion powder
- 1½ teaspoons garlic powder
- 1½ teaspoons dried basil
- 1½ teaspoons dried oregano
- 1 teaspoon salt
- 1 teaspoon dried thyme
- 1 teaspoon celery seed
- 1 teaspoon pepper
- 1 teaspoon cayenne pepper
- 1 bay leaf
- 12 ounces cream cheese, softened
- 1 tablespoon grated lime peel
- 2 tubes (11 ounces each) refrigerated crusty French loaf
- 2 cups (8 ounces) shredded Monterey Jack cheese

## Instructions

1. In a large saucepan, combine chicken, water, tomato paste, paprika, lime juice and seasonings. Bring to a boil and then reduce heat to low. Simmer, uncovered, for 20 minutes or until there is no more liquid, occasionally stirring. Discard the bay leaf.
2. Mix cream cheese and lime peel. On a large piece of foil, roll one tube of bread dough into a 14 inch x 10 inch rectangle. Spread with half of cream cheese mixture to within ½ inch of edges. Sprinkle with half of the chicken mixture and shredded cheese.

3. Fold into thirds, starting with a long side and using the foil. Form a 14 inch x 4 inch loaf with a seam along one side, pinching the edges to seal. Transfer to a baking sheet and repeat. Bake at 325°F for 45-50 minutes or until golden brown.
4. Remove from wire racks. Cool for 10 minutes before cutting into 1 inch slices. Place on a large serving platter and arrange to resemble ribs.

# Batwings

**SERVINGS:** 8-12
**PREP TIME:** 15 min. + marinating
**TOTAL TIME:** 1 hour

## Ingredients

- 2-3 pounds chicken wings, with tips
- 1 cup soy sauce
- 1/4 cup black bean sauce
- 1/4 cup tamarind paste (or oyster sauce)
- 1/4 cup brown sugar
- 1 Tablespoon chili garlic sauce
- 2 Tablespoons black food coloring (equal parts red, green, blue, yellow)

## Instructions

1. Mix all ingredients except chicken wings in a medium bowl and whisk well. Reserve 1/4 cup of this marinade for basting. Pour the rest of the marinade into a large plastic bag with the chicken wings and seal tightly.
2. Let the wings marinate in the refrigerator for 2 hours. Flip the bag of wings over every 30 minutes to ensure they get evenly coated.
3. Preheat oven to 375°F and line two baking sheets with parchment paper.
4. Remove wings from the bag of marinade and shake off extra marinade from the wings. Lay them on the baking sheets. Bake wings for 30-35 minutes until wings are dark black and cooked.
5. With the reserve marinade, baste wings once halfway through cooking and again when the wings come out.
6. Serve immediately.

# Slow Cooked Ghostly Beef Stew

**SERVINGS:** 6
**PREP TIME:** 30 min.
**TOTAL TIME:** 8 hours

## Ingredients

- 2 pounds beef stew meat, cut into 1-inch cubes
- 1 pound fresh mushrooms, halved
- 2 cups fresh baby carrots
- 2 medium parsnips, peeled, halved lengthwise and sliced
- 2 medium onions, chopped
- 1½ cups beef broth
- 3 tablespoons tomato paste
- 1 tablespoon Worcestershire sauce
- 2 garlic cloves, minced
- 1/2 teaspoon ground cloves
- 1/4 teaspoon pepper
- 8 medium potatoes (2⅓ pounds), peeled and cubed
- 2/3 cup sour cream
- 6 tablespoons butter, cubed
- 1 teaspoon salt, divided
- 1 cup frozen peas
- 2 tablespoons all-purpose flour
- 2 tablespoons water

## Instructions

1. In a 5 qt. slow cooker, combine all the first eleven ingredients listed, prior to the potatoes. Cover and cook on low for 8-9 hours or until beef and vegetables are tender.
2. 30 minutes prior to serving, place potatoes in a large saucepan and cover with water, bringing to a boil. Reduce heat, cover, and simmer for 15-20 minutes or until tender. Drain the water and return the potatoes to a pan, adding sour cream, butter and 1/2 teaspoon salt. Mash until smooth.
3. Set aside 12 peas for garnish, adding the remaining peas to the slow cooker. Increase heat to high. Whisk the flour, water and remaining

salt until smooth in a bowl and stir into stew. Cover and cook for 5 minutes or until thickened.

4. Divide stew among six bowls.
5. Place mashed potatoes in large resealable plastic bag and cut a 2 inch hole in the corner. Pipe ghost potatoes onto the stew. Place two reserved peas on each piped mash potato for eyes.

# Guts and Blood Potatoes

**SERVINGS:** 6-8
**PREP TIME:** 10 min.
**TOTAL TIME:** 2 hours

## Ingredients

- 4 baking potatoes
- 3 balls fresh mozzarella, diced
- 2 tablespoons tomato ketchup

## Instructions

1. Preheat the oven to 450 °F.
2. Prick potatoes with a fork and put into oven straight on the wire rack for 1 to 1½ hours or until baked.
3. Take potatoes out of the oven and let them cool. Slice each in half and scoop out potato flesh into a bowl, reserving the skins.
4. Place diced mozzarella into bowl with the potato and add the 2 tablespoons of ketchup. Mix with fork and spoon the filling back into the potato skins.
5. Place the potato skins on a lined baking sheet, and trickle more ketchup to make it look like bloody.
6. Place back in the oven and cook for 15 minutes, or until the cheese melts and the potatoes are warmed.

# Scary Eyeball Tacos

**SERVINGS:** 6-8
**PREP TIME:** 15 min.
**TOTAL TIME:** 55 min.

## Ingredients

- 1 lb ground beef
- 1 (1¼ ounce) package of taco seasoning mix
- 12 taco shells
- 3/4 cup salsa
- 3/4 cup sour cream
- 1 tomato cut in small cubes
- 1 small head lettuce, sliced into small confetti squares
- 1 (2¼ ounce) cans large black olives, sliced
- 1 cup cheese, shredded and long cheddar or Mexican blend

## Instructions

1. Mix beef and seasoning mix. Form half of the mixture into 24 balls, 1-inch around. Place in 15x10x1 inch baking pan and bake at 350°F for 15 to 20 minutes or until cooked.
2. Brown the remaining seasoned ground beef. Add salsa.
3. Fill each taco shell with a thin layer of ground beef, sour cream, lettuce, and tomatoes.
4. Place 2 meatballs inside the taco shell and add a drop of sour cream to each. Garnish with olives to make eyes. Spread the cheese along to the top of the taco for hair.

# Pea Soup with Black-Cat Croutons

**SERVINGS:** 8
**PREP TIME:** 20 min.
**TOTAL TIME:** 2 hours 20 min.

## Ingredients

- 8 rye bread slices, slightly stale
- 5 bacon slices
- 2 medium onions, chopped
- 2 large carrots, peeled and chopped
- 1 large celery rib, chopped
- 2 garlic cloves, minced
- 2 (32 oz.) cartons low-sodium chicken broth
- 1/2 cup water
- 1½ ups green split peas, rinsed
- 2 bay leaves
- 1 teaspoon dried thyme, crumbled
- 1½ teaspoons salt
- Freshly ground black pepper, to taste
- 1/2 cup sour cream

## Instructions

1. Preheat oven to 350°F. Remove crusts from stale bread slices. Brush bread on both sides with melted butter. With a knife cut out a cat shapes. Arrange on an ungreased cookie sheet.
2. Bake at 350°F for 15 minutes or until browned. Let cool.
3. Sauté bacon in large pot over medium-high heat until crisp and brown. Remove and set aside. Add onion, carrot and celery to pan and sauté until vegetables begin to soften. Add garlic and sauté for 1 minute. Add broth, water, peas, bay leaves and thyme and bring to a boil. Reduce heat to medium-low, partially cover pot and simmer until vegetables are tender and peas fall apart. Stir occasionally for 1 to 1½ hours.
4. Puree 5 cups of soup in batches in a blender and return to the pot. Sprinkle salt and season with pepper.

5. Ladle soup into serving bowls. Crumble reserved bacon on top. Add a cat crouton and a spoonful of sour cream to each bowl.

# Mouse Meatloaf

**SERVINGS:** 10
**PREP TIME:** 15 min.
**TOTAL TIME:** 1½ hours

## Ingredients

- 3 pounds ground beef
- 2 eggs
- 1 onion, chopped
- 2 cups milk
- 2 cups dry bread crumbs
- salt and ground black pepper to taste
- 1 (8 ounce) package shredded Cheddar cheese
- 3/4 (12 ounce) bottle barbeque sauce
- 1 cup French-fried onions
- 3 large black olives
- 3 spaghetti noodles, broken into halves
- 2 slices red potato
- 2 cups crushed French-fried onions

## Instructions

1. Preheat oven to 375°F.
2. Mix ground beef, eggs, onion, milk, bread crumbs, salt, and black pepper in a large bowl until completely combined.
3. Mix cheddar cheese, 3/4 bottle of barbeque sauce, and 1 cup French-fried onions in a separate bowl for the mouse guts.
4. Place half the ground beef mixture onto a sheet of waxed paper and form it into the shape of a mouse. Spread a thick layer of the cheesy mouse guts mixture on top of the body leaving 1/2 inch of space along the outer edge.
5. Put remaining meat mixture on top, forming the body and creating a solid seal around the edges so the guts don't come out while baking.
6. Place the top part of a broiler pan on the mouse and carefully flip over. Reshape body as needed. Place olives on for the eyes and nose, potato slices for the ears, and spaghetti for the whiskers. Spread ¼

bottle barbeque sauce over the mouse and sprinkle with crushed French-fried onions. Set the broiler rack atop the broiler pan.

7. Bake in preheated oven until the cheese is melted, about 1 hour. Allow the meatloaf to cool 5 minutes before slicing to serve.

# Maggot Pasta

**SERVINGS:** 8-12
**PREP TIME:** 15 min.
**TOTAL TIME:** 35 min.

## Ingredients

- 400g orzo pasta
- 2 tbsp. vegetable oil
- 2 red peppers, chopped
- 326g can sweetcorn, drained
- 175g frozen peas
- 3 garlic cloves, crushed
- 2 tsp five-spices
- 280g shredded ham
- 1 tbsp. soy sauce
- 220g jar black bean sauce
- 1 tbsp sesame oil

## Instructions

1. Cook the pasta using pack instructions. Drain, run under cold water, and drain again.
2. Heat the vegetable oil in a large pan or wok, add peppers, sweetcorn, peas, garlic and five-spice. Stir-fry for a few minutes. Add ham, soy sauce, 3/4 of the black bean sauce and the orzo, stir well and cook for 1-2 minutes. Stir in the sesame oil.
3. Heat the remaining black bean sauce in microwave. Place pasta into a large bowl and sprinkle over remaining sauce.

# Jack-O-Lantern Cheeseburger Pie

**SERVINGS:** 6-8
**PREP TIME:** 20 min.
**TOTAL TIME:** 45 min.

## Ingredients

- 1 pound ground beef
- 1 medium onion, chopped
- 2 garlic cloves, pressed
- 3/4 teaspoon salt
- 1/2 teaspoon pepper
- 1/4 cup ketchup
- 1 teaspoon Worcestershire sauce
- 1 (15-ounce) package refrigerated piecrusts
- 1 tablespoon prepared mustard
- 3 cups (12 ounces) shredded Monterey Jack cheese, divided
- 2 tablespoons water
- 1 large egg
- Red and yellow liquid food coloring

## Instructions

1. Cook first 5 ingredients in a large skillet over medium-high heat. Stir until beef crumbles and is no longer pink. Drain the water. Add ketchup and Worcestershire sauce. Let cool.
2. Unfold a piecrust, and place on a lightly greased baking sheet. Spread mustard evenly over crust. Stir meat mixture with 2 cups cheese and spoon onto the center of the piecrust while leaving a 2 inch border.
3. Unfold remaining piecrust, and cut out a jack-o'-lantern face. Set aside extra pie crusts to make a stem. Place crust over meat mixture, crinkle the edges of crust, and fold under. Place stem on top of the jack-o'-lantern face.
4. Whisk together 2 tablespoons water, egg, and 1 drop each of red and yellow food coloring. Brush over crust.
5. Bake at 425°F for 20 minutes. Remove from oven, and brush again with egg mixture. Fill eyes, nose, and mouth with remaining 1 cup of cheese. Bake 5 to 10 more minutes or until golden brown.

# Monster Booritos

**SERVINGS:** 8
**PREP/TOTAL TIME:** 25 min.

## Ingredients

- 1 envelope (5.6 ounces) Spanish rice and pasta mix
- 2 cups cubed cooked chicken
- 1 can (15 ounces) whole kernel corn, drained
- 1 can (14 ounces) diced tomatoes, drained
- 8 spinach tortillas (10 inches)
- For toppings: blue corn tortilla chips, cubed and shredded cheese, ripe olives and sweet red pepper
- Sour cream, optional

## Instructions

1. In a large saucepan, prepare rice mix according to package Instructions. Stir in chicken, corn and tomatoes and heat through.
2. Spoon about 2/3 cup rice mixture across center of each tortilla. Fold bottom and sides of tortilla over filling and roll up.
3. To create a face for each burrito, use blue tortilla chips for the hair, sweet red peppers cubed for the eyes, cubed cheese for the bolts on the neck, shredded cheese for the eyebrows, olive for the nose, and shredded cheese for the mouth.
4. Serve with sour cream if desired.

# Jack-O-Lantern Meat Pies

**SERVINGS:** 10
**PREP TIME:** 25 min.
**TOTAL TIME:** 1 hour

## Ingredients

- 1½ pounds ground beef
- 1 onion, chopped
- 1 tablespoon chili powder
- 1 teaspoon ground cumin
- 1/2 teaspoon salt
- 1/4 teaspoon garlic powder
- 1 (15 ounce) can tomato sauce
- 1 cup shredded carrot
- 1 (6 ounce) can chopped black olives, drained
- 1 (12 ounce) can refrigerated biscuit dough
- 10 slices American cheese

## Instructions

1. Preheat oven to 400°F. Grease 10 muffin cups.
2. Place ground beef and onion in a large skillet over medium heat. Cook and stir until the meat is browned and crumbly, about 10 minutes. Drain excess grease. Stir in the chili powder, cumin, salt, garlic powder, tomato sauce, carrot, and olives. Bring the mixture to a simmer. Cover the skillet, and cook until thickened and the carrot is tender, about 20 minutes. Stir occasionally.
3. On a floured surface, separate each biscuit, and roll out into 4 inch circles. Press the circles of biscuit dough into prepared muffin cups and bake in the preheated oven until the cups are lightly browned, about 10 minutes. Remove the biscuit cups from the pan, and place onto a baking sheet.
4. Cut the 10 slices of American cheese into 3-inch circles, and cut jack-o'-lantern faces into the circles with a paring knife. Chop remnants of cheese, and mix into the meat mixture. Fill the biscuit cups with meat mixture, and place a cheese face on top of each.

5. Return to the oven, and bake just until cheese begins to soften, 3 to 5 minutes.

# Spider Bread Loaf

**SERVINGS:** 16
**PREP TIME:** 30 min. + cooling
**TOTAL TIME:** 1½ hours

## Ingredients

- 2¼ to 2¾ cups all-purpose flour
- 1 tablespoon sugar
- 1 package (1/4 ounce) quick-rise yeast
- 1 teaspoon salt
- 1/2 cup water
- 1/3 cup milk
- 1 tablespoon butter
- 2 large eggs
- 2 raisins

## Instructions

1. In a large bowl, combine 2 cups flour, sugar, yeast and salt. In a small saucepan, heat the water, milk and butter to 120°-130°F. Add to dry ingredients and beat until moistened. Add 1 egg and beat until smooth. Stir in enough remaining flour to make the dough soft.
2. Turn onto a floured surface and knead until smooth and elastic, about 6-8 minutes. Cover and let rest for 10 minutes. Shape half of the dough into a ball and place in the center of a greased baking sheet. Divide remaining dough in half. Roll one half into a ball and place at the top for head.
3. Divide remaining dough into eight portions. Roll each into a 5 inch rope. Attach ropes to body, to form the legs. Press all edges together to seal. Add raisins to the head for eyes. Cover and let rise in a warm place until doubled, about 25 minutes.
4. Beat the remaining egg and brush over dough. With a sharp knife, make a shallow cut on face for the mouth. Bake at 350°F for 35-40 minutes or until golden brown. Remove to a wire rack to cool.

# Slithery Snake Calzone

**SERVINGS:** 12
**PREP TIME:** 20 min.
**TOTAL TIME:** 55 min.

## Ingredients

- 1 can (13.8 oz.) refrigerated pizza dough
- 1/2 cup Shredded Mozzarella Cheese
- 1/2 cup Ricotta Cheese
- 31 slices pepperoni, divided
- 1 egg white
- 1 drop each yellow and green food coloring, divided
- 2 manzanilla olives
- 1 cup pizza sauce

## Instructions

1. Preheat oven to 350°F.
2. Unroll dough on lightly floured work surface and roll or flatten to 17x10 inch rectangle. Combine cheeses.
3. Cut a pepperoni slice to resemble a snake's tongue and set aside. Arrange remaining pepperoni slices over dough rectangle, leaving 1 inch border around all sides. Top with spoonfuls of the cheese mixture. Roll up dough, starting at one long side and pinch seams together to seal. Place seam-side down, in the shape of an S on baking sheet sprayed with cooking spray to resemble snake.
4. Beat egg white and yellow food coloring lightly with fork. Brush half over dough. Add green food coloring to remaining egg white and brush randomly over dough to resemble a snake's skin. Insert olives into one end of dough for the snake's eyes. Add pepperoni tongue.
5. Bake 30 to 35 minutes or until golden brown.
6. Heat pizza sauce just until warmed.
7. Serve with the pizza sauce.

# Maggoty Worm Pasta

**SERVINGS:** 12
**PREP/ TOTAL TIME:** 25 min. + chilling

## Ingredients

- 8 ounces uncooked fusilli pasta or other spiral pasta
- 1 medium zucchini, julienned
- 1 cup cherry tomatoes
- 1 cup fresh cauliflowers
- 1 cup colossal ripe olives, halved
- 3/4 cup pimiento-stuffed olives
- 1 small green pepper, chopped
- 1/2 cup chopped red onion

DRESSING

- 1/4 cup ketchup
- 2 tablespoons sugar
- 2 tablespoons white vinegar
- 1/2 small onion, cut into wedges
- 1 garlic clove, peeled
- 1 teaspoon paprika
- 1/4 teaspoon salt
- 1/4 cup canola oil

## Instructions

1. Cook pasta according to package instructions. Drain and rinse in cold water. Place in a large bowl. Add the zucchini, tomatoes, cauliflower, olives, green pepper and red onion.
2. In a blender, combine the ketchup, sugar, vinegar, onion, garlic, paprika and salt. Cover and process until blended. While processing, gradually add oil in a steady stream, process until thickened. Pour over pasta salad and toss to coat.
3. Cover and refrigerate for at least 2 hours before serving.

# Bloody Corpse Meatloaf

**SERVINGS:** 10
**PREP TIME:** 30 min.
**TOTAL TIME:** 2 hours

## Ingredients

- 2 pounds ground beef chuck
- 1 pound bulk pork sausage
- 1 large onion, chopped
- 1 cup crushed saltine crackers
- 2 eggs, beaten
- 3 tablespoons Cajun seasoning
- 1 tablespoon corn kernels
- 2 pickle slices
- 3 black olives, halved
- 2 small slices of green bell pepper
- 2 cups ketchup

## Instructions

1. Preheat oven to 350°F.
2. Mix ground beef, sausage, onion, saltine cracker crumbs, beaten eggs, and Cajun seasoning in a bowl until well combined. In a large baking dish, form the meat loaf mixture into the basic shape of a person, with a head, 2 legs, and 2 arms.
3. Bake in the preheated oven until the meatloaf is no longer pink inside and just starting to turn brown, about 1 hour. An instant-read thermometer should read at least 165°F.
4. Place about 14 corn kernels and arrange them into teeth. Place 2 small green pepper slices on the creature's head for ears, two pickle slices for eyes, and 2 black olive halves, cut sides down, in the pickle slices for the iris. Add one more olive half for the nose. Surround with a background of ketchup and bake until browned, about 10 more minutes.
5. Let the meatloaf rest for 10 minutes before serving.
6. Before serving, stick a paring knife in the meatloaf's body, and add blood around the knife.

# Cooked Bats with Spider Webs

**SERVINGS:** 6
**PREP TIME:** 10 min.
**TOTAL TIME:** 40 min.

## Ingredients

- 1 (8 ounce) package farfalle (bow tie) pasta
- 1 pound ground beef
- 1 small onion, chopped
- 1 (28 ounce) jar pasta sauce
- 8 ounces mozzarella cheese, cut into 1/2 inch cubes
- 1/4 cup grated Parmesan cheese

## Instructions

1. Preheat oven to 400°F.
2. Fill a large pot with lightly salted water and bring to a rolling boil over high heat. Stir in the bow tie pasta and return to a boil. Boil pasta, occasionally stirring, until cooked through but still firm to the bite, about 12 minutes. Drain well.
3. Cook and stir ground beef and onion in a large skillet until beef is no longer pink, about 5 minutes. Drain fat. Stir in pasta sauce and bring to a boil. Reduce heat to simmer.
4. Stir cooked pasta and half of the mozzarella cheese into the sauce and toss to combine. Transfer to a 2 quart baking dish. Top with remaining mozzarella and Parmesan cheese.
5. Bake in preheated oven until lightly browned and bubbly, 15 to 20 minutes.
6. Serve warm.

# Monster Meatball Soup

**SERVINGS:** 4
**PREP/ TOTAL TIME:** 20 min.

## Ingredients

- 1 package (16 ounces) frozen fully-cooked beef meatballs
- 1 cup frozen vegetable mixture, such as broccoli, cauliflower and carrots
- 2 cups water
- 1 can (14 ounces) ready-to-serve beef broth
- 1 can (14 ounces) diced tomatoes with roasted garlic
- 3/4 cup uncooked Halloween pasta shapes

## Instructions

1. Combine frozen vegetables, water, broth, tomatoes and pasta in large saucepan and bring to a boil. Reduce heat and simmer 8 minutes or until pasta is just tender.
2. Microwave meatballs according to package directions. Add meatballs to soup, simmer 3 minutes or until meatballs are heated through. Garnish with Halloween decorations, if desired.

# Halloween Wild Rice in Pumpkin

**SERVINGS:** 4-6
**PREP TIME:** 30 min.
**TOTAL TIME:** 3½ hours

## Ingredients

- 1 package wild rice mix, cooked
- 1 pound breakfast pork sausage
- 1 pound lean ground beef
- 1 large onion, chopped
- Salt and pepper
- 1 cup celery
- 1 green bell pepper, chopped
- 1 can sliced water chestnuts
- 1 can (10.75 ounce size) cream of mushroom soup, undiluted
- 1 pumpkin, hollowed out

## Instructions

1. Cook rice according to package instructions
2. Brown meat and sauté vegetables. Add cooked rice, water chestnuts, soup, salt and pepper.
3. Place in pumpkin and cover with pumpkin top. Place in baking pan. Add water around bottom to keep from sticking. Bake at 350°F for 3 hours.

# Baked Rats

**SERVINGS:** 4-6
**PREP TIME:** 15 min.
**TOTAL TIME:** 1½ hours

## Ingredients

- 2 pounds ground beef
- 1/2 onion, chopped
- 1 egg, beaten
- 1 cup dry bread crumbs
- 1 (1.25 ounce) packet meatloaf seasoning mix
- 1 cup cubed Cheddar cheese
- 3 (10 ounce) cans tomato sauce
- 1 cup white sugar
- 1 tablespoon Worcestershire sauce
- 1 ounce uncooked spaghetti, broken into fourths
- 1/2 carrot, cut into 1/8 inch thick slices
- 1 tablespoon frozen green peas

## Instructions

1. Preheat oven to 350°F.
2. In a large bowl, combine the ground beef, onion, egg, bread crumbs, and meatloaf seasoning. Mix until well blended. Measure out 1/3 cupfuls of the meat mixture and mold a ball around a cube of cheese. Form a point at one end and lengthen the body by rolling between your hands to form a rat shape. Place into a shallow baking dish, and repeat with the remaining meat. Insert uncooked spaghetti pieces into the rounded end of the rats to make tails.
3. In a medium bowl, combine and mix the tomato sauce, sugar and Worcestershire sauce. Pour over the rats in the dish and cover with a lid or aluminum foil.
4. Bake for 45 minutes in the preheated oven. Uncover the dish and continue to bake for another 20 to 30 minutes, occasionally basting with the sauce to glaze the rats.
5. While the rats finish baking, heat the peas and carrots in a small bowl in the microwave for about 15 seconds.

6. Transfer the rats to a serving platter being careful so their tails don't come off. Press peas into the pointy end for eyes, and insert carrot slices for their ears. Spoon some of the tomato sauce around and serve.

# ***DESSERTS***

# Bloodshot Eyeballs

**SERVINGS:** 24
**PREP/TOTAL TIME:** 35 min. + chilling

## Ingredients

- 2 cups divided confectioners' sugar
- 1/2 cup creamy peanut butter
- 3 tablespoons softened butter
- 1/2 pound coarsely chopped white candy coating
- 24 brown Reese's pieces or milk chocolate M&M's
- 1 tablespoon water
- 1/4 to 1/2 teaspoon red food coloring

## Instructions

1. Combine 1 cup confectioners' sugar, peanut butter and butter in a small bowl. Form 1-in. balls and place on a waxed paper-lined pan. Chill for 30 minutes or until firm.
2. In a microwave, melt white candy coating and stir until smooth. Dip balls into the coating, allowing the excess to drip off and place on waxed paper. Immediately press a Reese's candy onto the top of each eyeball for pupil. Let stand for 30 minutes or until set.
3. Combine the water, food coloring and remaining confectioners' sugar in a small bowl. Transfer to a heavy-duty resealable plastic bag and cut a small hole into the corner of bag. Pipe wavy lines downward from pupil, to create bloodshot eyes. Store in an airtight container.

# Graveyard Dirt Pudding Parfait

**SERVINGS:** 8
**PREP/TOTAL TIME:** 20 min.

## Ingredients

- 1 (12 oz.) can evaporated milk
- 1 (15 oz.) can pumpkin puree (1¾ cup)
- 1 (5 oz.) box instant vanilla pudding
- 1 teaspoon cinnamon
- 1/2 an 8 oz. container cool whip
- 1 package Oreos, crushed
- 4 Tablespoons butter, melted
- 8 Milano cookies
- Handful chocolate chips

## Instructions

1. Combine evaporated milk, pumpkin puree, and pudding, and beat in a bowl of an electric mixer until smooth and well combined, about 2 minutes. Refrigerate for 5 minutes. Stir in cinnamon and cool whip. Refrigerate mixture until ready to serve.
2. In a bowl, combine melted butter and crushed Oreos. Set aside until ready to serve.
3. Place the Milano cookies up on a baking sheet or wax paper.
4. Melt the chocolate in the microwave then place it in a plastic bag. Cut a small hole in the corner of the plastic bag then push the chocolate to the corner.
5. Use the melted chocolate to write out RIP on the top of each of the cookies. Allow to dry.
6. When ready to serve, layer Oreos in the bottom of the glasses. Spoon pudding to about 3/4 of the way then finish with another layer of Oreos. Place the Milano cookies in the pudding mixture, with the RIP on top.

# Ghost Kisses

**SERVINGS:** 30
**PREP TIME:** 20 min. + standing
**TOTAL TIME:** 1 hour

## Ingredients

- 2 large egg whites
- 1/2 teaspoon vanilla extract
- 1/4 teaspoon almond extract
- 1/8 teaspoon cider vinegar
- 1/2 cup sugar
- Orange food coloring
- 1½ teaspoons miniature semisweet chocolate chips

## Instructions

1. In a small bowl, place egg whites and let stand at room temperature for 30 minutes. Add extracts and vinegar, beating on medium speed until soft peaks are formed. Gradually add 1 tablespoon at a time, beating in the sugar on high until sugar is dissolved and stiff glossy peaks form (about 6 minutes). Beat in the food coloring.
2. Cutting a small hole in the corner of a pastry or plastic bag, insert a #10 round pastry tip. Fill bag with egg white mixture. Pipe 1½ inch diameter ghosts onto parchment paper-lined baking sheets. Add two chips on each for eyes.
3. Bake at 250°F for 40-45 minutes or until set and dry. With the oven off, leave cookies in for 1 hour. Remove from parchment paper and store in an airtight container.

# Dracula Dentures

**SERVINGS:** 24
**PREP TIME:** 30 min.
**TOTAL TIME:** 40 min.

## Ingredients

- 1 package (18.25 ounces) refrigerated chocolate chip cookie dough
- 1/2 cup prepared vanilla frosting, tinted red
- 1¾ cups miniature marshmallows
- 48 (1 tablespoon) slivered almonds

## Instructions

1. Prepare cookies as directed on package or according to your favorite recipe. Cool on baking sheets for 2 minutes and remove to wire rack to cool. Cut each cookie in half for a total of 48 halves.
2. Spread the bottoms of all cookie halves with frosting. Place 6 marshmallow teeth around curved border of 24 halves and top with the remaining cookie halves. Place an additional marshmallow behind the teeth for support if needed. Dip the ends of two almond slivers into frosting and between marshmallows for fangs.

# Dirty Q-tips

**SERVINGS:** 10-20
**PREP/TOTAL TIME:** 20 min. + cooling

## Ingredients

- 20 white lollipop sticks
- 10 oz. miniature marshmallows
- 10 oz. chocolate or peanut butter chips

## Instructions

1. Cut down the lollipop sticks to Q-tip size, if necessary.
2. Push a miniature marshmallow onto each end.
3. Place a few peanut butter chips and a drizzle of milk in the microwave for 20-30 seconds, or until melted.
4. Dip the marshmallow ends into melted chocolate or peanut butter chips and lay them on some waxed paper to cool.

# Kitty Litter Cake

**SERVINGS:** 10-20
**PREP TIME:** 45 min.
**TOTAL TIME:** 1 hour

## Ingredients

- 1 (18.25 oz.) spice or German chocolate cake mix
- 1 (18.25 oz.) white cake mix
- 2 (3.5 oz.) packages vanilla instant pudding mix, prepared
- 1 (12 oz.) package vanilla sandwich cookies
- Green food coloring
- 1 (12 oz.) package small Tootsie Roll candies
- You'll also need:
- 1 new kitty litter pan
- 1 new kitty litter pan liner (or saran wrap)
- 1 new pooper scooper

## Instructions

1. Prepare and bake cake mixes according to Instructions.
2. Prepare pudding according to box Instructions and chill.
3. Crumble cookies in small batches in blender or food processor. Set aside all except 1/4 cup. To the 1/4 cup, add a few drops of green food coloring and mix.
4. When cakes are at room temperature, crumble them into a large bowl. Toss with half of the remaining cookie crumbs and enough chilled pudding to the mixture to make it moist but not soggy.
5. Place kitty litter liner, or saran wrap, in litter box and pour cake mixture into the litter box.
6. Unwrap 3 Tootsie Rolls and heat in a microwave until soft and pliable. Shape the ends into slightly curved points, until no longer blunt. Repeat with 3 more Tootsie Rolls and bury them randomly in the cake mixture.
7. Sprinkle the remaining white cookie crumbs over the mixture, then sprinkle a small amount of green crumbs lightly over top.

8. Heat 5 more Tootsie Rolls until almost melted. Scrape them on top of the cake and sprinkle with some of the green cookie crumbs.
9. Heat the remaining Tootsie Roll until pliable and same shape as before. Hang over the edge of the box, sprinkling with a few green cookie crumbs.
10. Serve with pooper scooper.

# Blood Clots

**SERVINGS:** 8-10
**PREP:** 20 min.
**TOTAL TIME:** 50 min.

## Ingredients

- 1 roll of Pillsbury flaky layers original biscuits
- 1 can of cherry pie filling
- 1/4 cup water
- Red food coloring
- Black food coloring

## Instructions

1. Pour the pie filling and water into a medium pan, and mush it up with a spoon to break up the cherries. Bring to a slow simmer and stir.
2. With a knife, cut each raw biscuit into 4 equal parts and roll into a ball.
3. Place some of the dough balls into the simmering pan with the pie filling. Sprinkle a few drops of red food coloring along with a few drops fewer of black food coloring. Cook them in batches so they have space to puff up.
4. Cover the pot, and let them simmer for about 15 minutes, or until they are puffed and frim. Check them every couple of minutes, to make sure they are cooking evenly.
5. Place in a bowl and serve.

# Eye-Scream

**SERVINGS:** 8
**PREP/TOTAL TIME:** 30 min.

## Ingredients

- 1 quart vanilla ice cream
- Strawberry syrup (such as Hershey's)
- 8 M&M's (blue, green or brown)
- Black decorating gel

## Instructions

1. Scoop ice cream into balls and place on wax-paper-lined cookie sheet. Place in freezer until ready to serve (at least 20 minutes).
2. Place ice cream balls on a serving plate when ready to serve.
3. Drizzle syrup on each ball to create a bloodshot veins. Put an M&M chocolate with the logo facing down in the center of each ball and place a drop of black decorating gel for the pupils.

# Maggot and Worm Apples

**SERVINGS:** 6
**PREP/ TOTAL TIME:** 20 min.

## Ingredients

- 6 apples
- ½ juiced lemon
- 3.5 ounces of white chocolate
- 1.5 ounces of puffed rice
- Jelly worms (optional)

## Instructions

1. Core apples, but keep the stalk ends intact. Use a skewer and make 1 or 2 holes in the sides. Brush the cut apple parts with lemon juice and place on a plate.
2. In a heatproof bowl, place chocolate over a pan of simmering water until melted. Stir in puffed rice, then remove from the heat. Pack the chocolate and puffed rice mixture into the apples with a teaspoon, sticking a few into the smaller holes and on the top to look like they're crawling out. Transfer to fridge for 20 mins to set.
3. Spoon remaining mixture into a mini muffin tin lined with paper petit four cases. Place in fridge to set along with the apples.
4. Once chocolate has set, peel away paper cases and place the 'maggot balls' around the apples. Add a few wriggly jelly worms to the apples.

# Terrifying Sweet Fingers

**SERVINGS:** 30
**PREP:** 25 min. + chilling
**TOTAL TIME:** 45 min.

## Ingredients

- 1 cup butter, softened
- 1 cup confectioners' sugar
- 1 egg
- 1 teaspoon vanilla extract
- 1 teaspoon almond extract
- 2¾ cups all-purpose flour
- 1 teaspoon baking powder
- 1 teaspoon salt
- Red decorating gel
- 1¾ cup sliced almonds

## Instructions

1. Place the cream butter and sugar in a large bowl. Beat in the egg and extracts. Combine the flour, baking powder and salt; gradually adding it to the creamed mixture. Divide dough into quarters. Cover and refrigerate for 30 minutes or until easy to handle.
2. Roll each piece of dough into 1 inch balls. Shape balls into 3 inches x 1/2 inches fingers. Use the flat tip of a table knife and make an indentation on one end of each for the fingernail. Make three slashes in the middle of each finger for knuckle.
3. Place the fingers 2 inches apart on lightly greased baking sheets. Bake at 325°F for 20-25 minutes or until lightly browned. Cool for 3 minutes. Squeeze a small amount of red gel for nail and press a sliced almond over gel to represent the nail, allowing the gel to secrete underneath. Remove wire racks to cool.

# Giant Ogre Toes

**SERVINGS:** 22
**PREP/ TOTAL TIME:** 25 min. + standing

## Ingredients

- 12 ounces white candy coating, coarsely chopped
- Green paste food coloring
- 22 Nutter Butter cookies
- 11 black dots or Crows candies, halved lengthwise

## Instructions

1. In a microwave, melt the candy coating and stir until smooth. Add green food coloring.
2. Dip cookies into candy coating. Let excess drip off and place on waxed paper. Immediately place a candy half, cut side down, on each cookie to represent the toe nails.
3. Let stand for 15 minutes or until set.

# Chocolate Mice

**SERVINGS:** 6-8
**PREP TIME:** 20 min. + refrigerating
**TOTAL TIME:** 2 hours 20 min.

## Ingredients

- 4 (1 ounce) semi-sweet chocolate baking squares
- 1/3 cup sour cream
- 1 cup chocolate wafer, finely crushed
- 1/3 cup additional chocolate wafer, finely crumbled
- 1/3 cup confectioners' sugar
- 24 silver dragees
- 24 sliced almonds
- 12 (2 inch) liquorice, strings

## Instructions

1. Melt the chocolate and combine with sour cream and 1 cup of the chocolate wafer crumbs, mixing well. Cover and refrigerate until firm.
2. Roll by level tablespoonful into balls, and create a slight point at one end to create the nose.
3. Roll dough in confectioners' sugar for white mice; and chocolate wafer crumbs for black mice.
4. On each mouse, place dragees in appropriate spot for eyes, almond slices for ears, and a liquorice string for the tail.
5. Refrigerate for two hours or until firm.

# Banana Ghosts

**SERVINGS:** 8
**PREP/TOTAL TIME:** 10 min. + refrigeration

## Ingredients

- 7 ounces white chocolate bar
- 4 medium-large ripe bananas
- 3 ounces desiccated coconut
- Handful of dark chocolate drops

## Instructions

1. In a small bowl, melt the chocolate over a pan of simmering water making sure the bowl doesn't touch the water or in the microwave on HIGH in short bursts.
2. Peel the bananas, cut in half, and push a wooden stick in the middle of each half.
3. Spread coconut out in a shallow bowl. Line a large baking tray with parchment paper.
4. Coat a banana half in chocolate with a pastry brush, letting the excess drip off. Sprinkle with coconut until coated, and set it on the prepared sheet. Add two chocolate eyes and a mouth, and cut a few little eyebrows from the chocolate drops. Freeze for at least 4 hrs, and up to a week.

# Vampire Mouth Pies

**SERVINGS:** 14
**PREP TIME:** 30 min.
**TOTAL TIME:** 45 min.

## Ingredients

- 1 package (14.1 ounces) refrigerated pie pastry
- 3 ounces cream cheese, softened
- 1/3 cup walnut or peanut butter
- 1 large egg, beaten
- 1/2 cup sugar
- 1/2 cup cranberry juice
- 1½ cups fresh or frozen cranberries, thawed
- Miniature marshmallows

## Instructions

1. Unroll pastry on a floured surface. Using a 3 inch round cutter, cut out seven circles from each sheet. Place 1/2 teaspoon of cream cheese and 1/2 teaspoon walnut or peanut butter in the center of each pastry. Brush egg around edges. Fold pastry over pressing down around filling to seal. Brush tops with egg.
2. Transfer to ungreased baking sheets. Bake at 400°F for 13-15 minutes or until golden brown. Cool for 1 minute before removing from pans to wire racks.
3. In a small saucepan, combine sugar and juice. Bring to a boil and cook until liquid is thick and syrupy. Remove from the heat and cool slightly. Place cranberries in a blender. Cover and process until chopped. Add syrup and process until smooth.
4. Cut marshmallows diagonally in half to look like fangs. When pastries are cool enough, pry open slightly and dip in syrup to resemble blood. Add fangs.

# Frankenstein Cookies

**SERVINGS:** 24
**PREP/TOTAL TIME:** 40 min. + chilling + cooling

## Ingredients

- 1 package (17½ ounces) sugar cookie mix
- 1 tablespoon all-purpose flour
- 1/2 cup butter, melted
- 1 egg
- 1 teaspoon vanilla extract
- 1/4 teaspoon peppermint extract
- 5 drops green food coloring
- 24 Andes mint candies
- Black and white jimmies
- Decorating icing

## Instructions

1. In a large bowl, combine cookie mix and flour. Stir in melted butter, egg, extracts and food coloring until blended.
2. Shape into a 6 inch long roll and wrap in plastic wrap. Refrigerate for an hour. Unwrap and shape roll into a square-shaped log using wax paper. Freeze 30 minutes or until firm.
3. Preheat oven to 350°F. Unwrap and cut log crosswise into 1/4 inch slices. Place 1 inch apart on parchment paper-lined baking sheets. Place one mint candy onto top of each square and sprinkle with jimmies for the hair. Bake 10-12 minutes or until edges are light brown. Remove from pans to wire racks to cool completely.
4. Decorate faces as desired with icing.

# Slimy Worm Dessert

**SERVINGS:** 8
**PREP/ TOTAL TIME:** 20 min. + chilling

## Ingredients

- 1 package of lime or apple Jell-O
- 1 package of cherry, berry-blue or grape Jell-O\
- 1 package of gummy worms

## Instructions

1. Prepare a package of lime or apple Jell-O according to package instructions. Divide liquid among 8 mason jars or clear bowls, filling each halfway. Refrigerate until firm.
2. Prepare another Jell-O flavor, such as cherry, berry-blue or grape according to package instructions. While Jell-O is cooking, place three gummy worms on top of set gelatin and let another hang over the lip. Pour second flavor over the worms and fill to the top. Refrigerate.

# Red Hot Ghosts

**SERVINGS:** 4-6
**PREP/ TOTAL TIME:** 15 min.

## Ingredients

- 1 cup white-chocolate chips
- 1 tablespoons vegetable shortening
- 8 large marshmallows
- 6 wooden skewers, points cut off
- 12 cinnamon Red Hots
- Black decorating gel

## Instructions

1. Microwave white-chocolate and shortening in a microwave-safe dish on medium-high for 1 minute. Stir. Microwave in 10 second intervals until smooth
2. Push three marshmallows onto end of skewer. Holding the skewer, spoon the melted mixture over marshmallows until covered. Place on wax-paper-lined cookie sheet. Use two Red Hots for eyes and decorating gel for a mouth.
3. Refrigerate until chocolate is hard.

# Spider Brownies

**SERVINGS:** 9
**PREP TIME:** 20 min. + cooling
**TOTAL TIME:** 1 hour

## Ingredients

- 1 package fudge brownie mix (8 inch square pan size)
- 1/2 cup semisweet chocolate chips
- 2 cups crispy chow mein noodles
- 18 candy eyeballs

## Instructions

1. Prepare and bake brownies according to package using an 8 inch square baking pan lined with parchment paper. Cool completely in pan on a wire rack.
2. In a microwave, melt chocolate chips and stir until smooth. Remove 1 tablespoon melted chocolate to a small bowl. Set aside. Add noodles to remaining chocolate and stir gently to coat. Spread onto a waxed paper-lined baking sheet, separating noodles slightly. Freeze until set.
3. Cut nine brownies with a 2¼ inch round cutter for the body of the spider. Attach eyeballs using the melted chocolate that was set aside. With a bamboo skewer or toothpick, poke eight holes in top of each spider for inserting legs. Insert a coated noodle into each hole. Store in an airtight container.

# ***DRINKS***

# Boo Beverage

**SERVINGS:** 9
**PREP/TOTAL TIME:** 15 min.

## Ingredients

- 2 cups orange juice
- 2 cups milk
- 2 pints orange sherbet
- 4 medium ripe bananas
- 2 cups whipped topping
- 18 miniature semisweet chocolate chips

## Instructions

1. In batches of four, blend the orange juice, milk, sherbet and bananas in a blender until smooth. Pour into glasses.
2. Cut a hole in the corner of a pastry or plastic bag and fill with whipped topping. Pipe a ghost shape on top of each beverage, and place chocolate chips for the eyes.

# Eyeball Punch

**SERVINGS:** 8
**PREP/TOTAL TIME:** 20 min. + freezing + chilling

## Ingredients

- 1/2 pint blueberries
- 1 qt. water
- Yellow food coloring
- 1 1/4 cups fresh lemon juice
- 1/2 cup fine sugar
- 1 cup orange juice or orange liqueur, if alcoholic
- 1/4 cup cranberry juice or raspberry liqueur, if alcoholic
- 2 liters of ginger ale or 2 (750 ml) bottles dry Champagne, if alcoholic, chilled
- 2 lemons, thinly sliced, for garnish

## Instructions

1. Place a blueberry in each compartment of iceball tray. Mix 1 quart of water with few drops of food coloring. Fill tray and freeze overnight.
2. Combine lemon juice, sugar, and orange and raspberry juice or liqueurs in a pitcher. Stir until sugar is dissolved. Cover and chill for 1 hour.
3. Pour lemon juice mixture into punch bowl. Mix with ginger ale or champagne and stir. Add lemon slices and frozen blueberry eyeballs to bowl.
4. Serve in long stemmed glasses.

# Slimy Worm-Ade

**SERVINGS:** 6
**PREP/TOTAL TIME:** 15 min.

## Ingredients

- 2 cups white grape juice
- 2 cups apple juice
- 12 to 15 drops neon-green food coloring
- 4 to 7 drops neon-blue food coloring
- 2 cups seltzer
- 1/4 cup light corn syrup
- 6 to 12 gummy worms

## Instructions

1. Mix grape and apple juices in a pitcher. Add 10 to 12 drops neon-green food coloring, and 3 to 5 drops neon-blue food coloring. Stir. Add seltzer and set aside.
2. Pour corn syrup into a small bowl, wide enough to fit the rim of a glass. Stir in 2 to 3 drops neon-green food coloring, and 1 to 2 drops neon-blue coloring.
3. Dip the rims of 6 glasses into syrup.
4. Fill each glass with the juice/seltzer mixture. Stick gummy worms to the slimy syrup.

# Bloody Vampire Alcoholic Cocktail

**SERVINGS:** 1
**PREP/TOTAL TIME:** 5 min.

## Ingredients

- 1 scoop vanilla ice cream
- 1 oz. triple sec
- 1/2 oz. white crème de cacao
- Drizzle of grenadine

## Instructions

1. Blend all ingredients except grenadine until smooth and pour into a cocktail glass.
2. Drizzle grenadine on top of the drink.

# Bloody Punch

**SERVINGS:** 8
**PREP/TOTAL TIME:** 15 min. + chilling

## Ingredients

- 3 oranges or blood oranges
- 1 (64 oz.) bottle cranberry juice cocktail
- 1 quart chilled orange juice
- 1 cup chilled vodka
- 1/2 cup triple sec
- 3 tablespoons fresh lime juice

## Instructions

1. Cut the oranges into 1/2 inch wedges and freeze.
2. In a pitcher or punch bowl, mix the cranberry juice cocktail, chilled orange juice, chilled vodka, triple sec and fresh lime juice. For non-alcoholic drinks leave out the vodka and triple sec.
3. Serve with the frozen orange wedges.

# Brain Ooze Alcoholic Cocktail

**SERVINGS:** 1
**PREP/TOTAL TIME:** 5 min.

## Ingredients

- 1½ oz. peach schnapps
- 1½ oz. Baileys Irish cream
- Dash of grenadine

## Instructions

1. Pour peach schnapps into a glass.
2. Add Baileys Irish cream slowly.
3. Top the drink with a splash of grenadine.

# Severed Hand Sangria

**SERVINGS:** 10
**PREP/TOTAL TIME:** 15 min. + freezing

## Ingredients

- 1 or more Latex gloves
- 32 oz. filtered water
- 2 bottles dry red wine
- 3 cups sparkling water
- 3 cups freshly squeezed orange juice
- 3 oz. brandy (or Cointreau)
- 3 tbsp. brown sugar
- 2 fresh oranges, thinly sliced
- 2 fresh pink grapefruit, thinly sliced
- 2 fresh lemons, thinly sliced
- 2 fresh limes, thinly sliced
- 1 cup natural sour cherries in syrup

## Instructions

1. The night before serving, fill as many latex gloves as desired with filtered water. Tie up the ends and freeze overnight.
2. In a large punch bowl combine red wine, sparkling water, orange juice, brandy, brown sugar, fruit slices, and sour cherry syrup. Stir.
3. Remove the latex glove from the freezer, take out the ice-hand and add to the Sangria.
4. For a kid friendly fruit punch, remove the alcohol ingredients.

# Vampire Blood Punch

**SERVINGS:** 12
**PREP/TOTAL TIME:** 15 min + chilling

## Ingredients

- 2 liters of cherry juice
- Peels from 3 oranges, pared with a vegetable peeler
- 1 thumb-sized red chilli, pierced a few times
- 3 cinnamon sticks
- 10 cloves
- 6 ginger, slices
- Dracula's fangs sweets, optional

## Instructions

1. Combine cherry juice, orange peel, chilli, cinnamon sticks, cloves and ginger into a large saucepan. Simmer for 5 minutes. Turn off the heat, leave to cool. Place in the refrigerator and chill for at least 4 hours or up to 2 days. If desired, take the chilli out after a few hours so it's not too spicy for children.
2. Pour the juice into a jug, when ready to serve. Place Dracula's fangs sweet into each glass.

# Witches Brew

**SERVINGS:** 20
**PREP/ TOTAL TIME:** 15 min.

## Ingredients

- 1 gallon orange sherbet, softened
- 1 quart pineapple juice, chilled
- 1 liter carbonated lemon-lime beverage

## Instructions

1. Combine sherbet and pineapple juice in a punch bowl and stir well.
2. Add soda and stir until sherbet is nearly dissolved.
3. Serve punch immediately.

# Bloody Lime Sherbet

**SERVINGS:** 4
**PREP/ TOTAL TIME:** 20 min.

## Ingredients

- 4 cups of apple juice
- 3 tbsps. light corn syrup
- 2-4 drops red food coloring
- 3/4 quart lime sherbet, softened
- 1½ cups pink grapefruit juice
- 1½ cups club soda
- Vodka, if alcoholic

## Instructions

1. Combine corn syrup and red food coloring in a shallow dish wider that the rim of your glasses. Mix until corn syrup is completely red.
2. In a blender, combine lime sherbet, pink grapefruit juice and club soda. Add vodka to taste if alcoholic. Blend until frothy and fully combined, about 10 seconds.
3. Dip the rim of each glass into the red corn syrup. Turn each glass upright and let the corn syrup drip down the sides.
4. Pour the punch into the glasses and serve.

# Black Death Punch

**SERVINGS:** 12
**PREP/TOTAL TIME:** 10 min

## Ingredients

- 1 (.13 ounce) envelope unsweetened grape soft drink mix
- 1 (.13 ounce) envelope unsweetened orange soft drink mix
- 2 cups white sugar
- 3 quarts cold water
- 1 liter ginger ale or 750 mL of champagne, if alcoholic

## Instructions

1. Stir together grape soft drink mix, orange soft drink mix, sugar and water until solids are dissolved. Combine with chilled ginger ale, or just before serving.

# Floating Faces Punch

**SERVINGS:** 8
**PREP/ TOTAL TIME:** 20 min. + chilling

## Ingredients

- 4 cups of apple juice
- 4 cups of red wine, or cranberry juice if non-alcoholic
- Pinch of cinnamon
- Pinch of nutmeg
- 8 medium-sized apples
- 2 tablespoons of brown sugar

## Instructions

1. Mix apple juice with red wine or cranberry juice.
2. Peel apples and remove seeds. Cut in half and carve into a round ball. Cut eyes, mouth, and nose with knife.
3. Drop apple heads into drink mixture and add sugar and spices.
4. Chill and serve in large bowl.

# ***THANK YOU***

Thank you for checking out my Halloween Cookbook. I hope you enjoyed these recipes as much as I have. I am always looking for feedback on how to improve, so if you have any questions, suggestions, or comments please send me an email at susan.evans.author@gmail.com. Also, if you enjoyed the book would you consider leaving on honest review? As a new author, they help me out in a big way. Thanks again, and have fun cooking!

Other popular books by Susan Evans

Vegetarian Slow Cooker Cookbook:
*Over 75 recipes for meals, soups, stews, desserts, and sides*

Quick & Easy Asian Vegetarian Cookbook:
*Over 50 recipes for stir fries, rice, noodles, and appetizers*

Vegetarian Mediterranean Cookbook:
*Over 50 recipes for appetizers, salads, dips, and main dishes*

Quick & Easy Vegan Desserts Cookbook:
*Over 80 delicious recipes for cakes, cupcakes, brownies, cookies, fudge, pies, candy, and so much more!*

Quick & Easy Vegetarian Rice Cooker Meals:
*Over 50 recipes for breakfast, main dishes, and desserts*

Quick & Easy Rice Cooker Meals:
*Over 60 recipes for breakfast, main dishes, soups, and desserts*

Quick & Easy Microwave Meals:
*Over 50 recipes for breakfast, snacks, meals and desserts*

Made in the USA
Lexington, KY
21 September 2017